State of Being

Poems by C. R. Dyer

To Howard —
a fellow-lover
of poetry
CRDyer

ISBN 978-1-475141-88-7

Manufactured in the United States of America

Cover and text illustrations by C. R. Dyer.

In memory of my husband,
Clarence R. Dyer
and 60 years of lively conversation

Flow of Contents

Morning Sleep
Muse
Poetry
Writer
Reading
Arts

State of Being
Brain
Memories

Where am I going?
Advice and Observations
Daily
Brief Pics
Food
Nature

Couples
Bus
Last Thoughts
Oddities

The dawn crowed violently in my ear,
Then pierced my flutter-opened eyes,
Sent me diving in denial
To the blanketed burrow of my caved-in mattress,
Where I crouched in the cruel futility of hope.
But no. The slightly-muted morning racket
Drilled through my paltry defenses.
Emptied suddenly of Morpheus' balm,
I arose, begrudgingly,
To the strident music of the morning.

Nested in Morpheus' balm
Lurked the insidious nightmare
Awaiting the droop of eyelids.

Killing Time
My mornings come in 30-minute pieces
Of half-o-clocks.
Sterile spans,
Characterized
By pill-punctuated ends,
The in-betweens dead as hair strands,
Functioning simply to separate
The taking-of—

Don't bay at the moon. Go to sleep!
(The moon doesn't care
Unless you're a wolf—
They have an understanding.)

My bedroom gnat
Shanghaied the remote
With a four-itemed menu
That never sleeps.

My timer, Speedy the Defunct,
Has run out of spunk,
Doing double-quick time,
Hours ticked
Into 30-minute segments;
Take a lesson
From my adrenalized pal:
Stroll the garden.

So wrenching to leave the coziness
Of a familiar pillow
For the bugle call
Of duty.

The pursuit in an oarless dream
Landed her awake
On a familiar, emotional sandbar
Heart pounding
At the fraud of escape.

I so enjoy finally snuggled
In a deep sleep,
I pinch myself awake
Not to miss it.

I dropped out of the room,
Napped some sudden seconds
At a small table,
Completely plunged
Into a corner of life
Oh so private,
Not a "where" place.
Eyes still closed,
I tried to guess
Where I had dropped from.
A Lovely Snooze

In the dreams of night,
I recognize my days,
Shuffled pieces oddly juxtaposed.

Agenda
I lightly sketch in
Some naps for the day
As soon as I leave
My morning bed.

I can hardly wait
To get out of bed in the morning,
So I can take a nap.

The crawl around the dial—
Still no sleep.

In the crowded day
I leapfrog
Over hours of erased memory
To the other side of the clock.
Darn! Forgot my pills again.

She fought the rhythm in her head,
Pulsing loud and commandeering
In the creature instrument.
She whirred a failed flutter
Counterpuntal to its throb;
If once she could escape it,
She would tell and tell and tell.

If I could sleep faster,
Waking at 2 a.m. wouldn't be so bad.
A rooster crows violently
Inside my head
In before-the-sun hours.
Lying in the failed haven
Of my darkened bedroom,
The question jabs:
What to do in a four-hour patch
With the congregation
Of agitating company
Clanging in my brain—
Errant thoughts, tipsy with nonsense,
Or maybe with too much sense to bear.
I have no controlling remote
To shift out of the problems
To deal with today,
And today, and today...
It's still today?

Oh Morpheus,
You desert me.
Bereft of your soothing nourishment,
I'd been left to stumble
In famished daze
Until an unemployed Muse
Spotted an opportunity
To tamper.

Don't bend, begging,
To a haughty, withholding Muse;
Rather, invite the gift
With openness,
And your promised industry
In creative application.

Some lost, wandering foreign muse
Happened upon my ear.
Its utterances claimed my hand.
The words penned on the page
Sent me to my mirror
To see if the image
Were familiar.

My muse, the whisperer,
Allows me to claim as my own
The words that shout in my brain

Awake, my sleeping muse
In my slumbering brain,
So I, at the new day,
Find astonishing words
On the hungry page.

I, the conduit for an impatient muse,
Writhe in the awkward birth
Of words,
Astonished at their appearance
On the page.

The restless muse
Looks to my pen
For relief.

Beware the contagion
Of a demented muse.

The acrid tongue of my muse
Makes me cranky, too.

My muse is no longer languid
But prodding in sudden industry
That I must match
To scratch the need

Did some exhausted poet
Fire his muse
And send to me, unwittingly, to hire?

The poem is an acorn
Tightly wrought,
Inviting the invigorating sap
Of the reader's imagination
To spring clasping roots
Bark-y trunk, reaching branches,
Breezed leaves rustling,
A rightful place for twitters and tweets
Of attendant birds,
Arboreal architects
With a nestful
Of miniature maws,
Skyward-open in confident appetite—
A sighing, leaning lover
Gazing upward through the lacery—
The reader's story
Curls out of the acorn.

Metaphors—
The closest we can get
To the ungraspable.
Would you want
A universe
In its vastness
Completely understandable
By the tiny human brain?

The seasonal bier
Of autumn leaves
Quotes philosophical musings
In its smoke.

The words,
Strung in the beaded-speak
Of poetry,
Glistened in her mind,
The dew of each morning's wake.

Examining a poem
Is like handling a magical gadget
Which mists beyond itself.

Out of my time?!
I've used only one
"For the nonce"
In all my poetry.

The poem
An abstraction with bones
For you to dress
From the closet
Of your experiences

The poem was an island on the page,
A cluster of words
That gravitates the eye,
Captures the mind
With a reminding thought
Slowly nuanced back
Into some faintly familiar
Original knowledge

A good poem
Can send you deep within yourself
Past the prose of daily life.

Writer's Dream
Words threshed by wind into confetti
Whirled—the cloudful eddied
Above his head in his front yard.
The cloud burst and rained down
The celebratory flakes.
He raised welcoming arms,
Head flung back, tongue thrust forward
Like a ladle, to capture the manna.
To deny the wind, he raked the leaves,
Scooped them into a wheelbarrel.
With trembling hands,
Trundled the prize into the house,
Tilted the leaves unto his desk.
He sprinkled a handful onto the page.
Brilliant yellows, reds, oranges
Tumbled down,
Turned to sepia on contact.
The failed froth of his effervescence
Flattened
In the morning wake.

The Refurbisher
He deployed the word
Into broader employment.
It brightened considerably
With restored vigor
In the friction of new context
And startled unexpected companions
To unanchored possibilities—
Shook trees loose
Of their "twitters" and "tweets,"
Delved hearts for "ugly blessings,"
Trembled in vibration
To "clamorous silence."

Words crackle in the mind,
Edges sharp,
Crevises shadowed with nuance
Inviting delving – later.
Always,
A row of wadded paper snowballs,
Shelved for the nonce,
Waits deliciously
For his moments of full fertility
To indulge the one-time unfolding
Unto the hungry blank page.

A haiku's worth of
Original syllables
Fits in my coin purse.

He writes
Pre-fab litter-(ature).

She paginates blank leaves,
Hoping for the return
Of the inventive muse.

The words are piled high
Against the closet door.
All I need do
Is turn the knob
And pull;
They'll fall into the room,
Alphabet blocks.
I sit on the floor and build.

Oddly-companioned words
Each animate the other
At a new slant
In widened repertoire.

Don't go code on me
With your arcane lingo.

Not every slope is slippery
As your tongue.

A pile of piths
Rolled tightly,
Ready for the reader
To unfold
With his own recognizables
In the creases.

"Um...uh..." she stuttered,
Starved for vocabulary.

The clatter and the clank,
The hum and the buzz
The sss and the boom,
The frizzle and the thud
The shriek and the whine
The burble and the whoosh,
The ... (Your turn)

I don't want to sound pedestrian,
Stilted or generic
('Though doing so has its place,
Hiding who-knows-what).

Inky tails of careless strokes
Bespoke a hasty pen.

I wrote the book
To find out by reading it
The nature of my mind.

Artful metaphors
Could not hide
The rawness of the fact.

I do not force the simmering idea:
I nudge and wait.
A word, a phrase
Will dance forth—
A tap dance, a waltz,
A stroll of thought,
A few lines
Package themselves.
I take it from there,
Sing the rest.

Metaphors stream naturally,
Atmospherically,
Bedecking each occasion.

The literal mind
Suffocated the real truth
Of the spirited metaphor.

In that witching hour
Fringed around 3 A.M.
An emboldened pen
Lurches awake.

Alone but not lonely,
My fired-up pen
Is the only company I need.

A voice recorder?
Don't encourage me.
I'm already talking to myself.

My drunken pen
Lurches on
Undeterred
By a drought
Of any sense.

Blank pages, austere to the ultimate
Both forbidding and daring
The nervous pen,
The writer's quell
Of trepidation—
To Word.

Reaching toward the lamp switch,
My hand fell upon the book
As yet unopened,
So still an object
Beside my bed,
Unobtrusive to invisibility,
The voice inside waiting.
This morning, I opened it
To page after page
Bursting with a lively mind
That woke mine
In hallowed exchange.

The complete reader
Travels the poem,
As richly read as wrought:
The artist audience.

All the people
I've read alive!
Words, minds, characters
Pulse through my senses
As fully as if standing beside—
Oh, what I would have missed
To have let stay shelved
For "Some day",
A life away.

The libraries in my head
Finally sought out an available pen
And thrust it into my hand.

After 15 minutes
I put down the book
An hour later.

Page 27 is just the other side
Of this leaf;
Now to separate stuck-together pages,
A delicate operation
For fumbling thumbs,
And a bumbling mind
Searching for answers

Sit in any corner:
On a chair
Or on a bed,
On the floor
Or on a step,
On a branch
Or in a car,
A turn of page transports you
To another place.

Can I scrape up an intensity
That isn't there?
I often read my way to that state,
Break open a book
Of a flourishing mind.
In my drought and in my thirst,
Delicious energies
Soothe and ignite.

She sipped at the book
In leisurely pace
A few pages,
Then a gathering of two minds
In conversational pause—
Sip and pause, sip and pause.
Refurbished
She put down the empty cup,
And closed the book.

The Room Next Door
We lead parallel lives,
We book readers.
With a fingered tip off the shelf
Of a beloved volume,
We step into another room.

On reading Greene
I chug slowly through the ideas
In industrious efforts
To digest their profundities,
In sips of starts and stops
And back-ups and reruns.
Rewarded in sudden exhilarating,
Epiphanal gulps of amazement—
At discoveries new
Yet strangely familiar,
Resonating in a song
Old as the universe—
Recognizable by every soul
Who dares the interior journey
To vastness.

Night Reading
From the bed
I noted one drawer ajar,
The slit seeping a darkness
From inside.
Like a picture on a wall,
Hanging askew,
Not straightened home,
The incompleteness nagged,
Brought to mind
Some other task left ajar,
Lost in the crowded day,
Its unpleasantness
Still unsettled.
I couldn't read it away,
But nimbus-like,
Over my head it hung.
Finding no distracting retreat,
Reluctantly, I left the bed
And shut the darn thing.
It didn't help!
I lay there, thumb in place,
Tapping a finger
On the table top of the book,
Trying to rein in my roused thoughts.

A voice from another acoustic
Chambered within her
Gave pause to her thoughts,
Stretched them
In elastic rubato,
Reminded of some lost original knowledge,
A delicate echo,
A shadow of sound.

AFTER THE BALL
Blissfully she swayed, dipped,
Swivelled, stepped intricately,
Soared in the lavishness
Of the dream—
Then fell, stumbled into consciousness
To frozen feet resting on pedals,
Arms heavily draped,
Hands dangling over idle wheels.
"Awake me dead!
Please awake me dead instead!"

They baptized the chamber
With the first song,
Afresh with celebration—
The reverberating wash of sound
Its initial patina.

The Sunday soaring
Of glad choirs
Gave voice
To the singing angels
Painted on the vaulted ceiling
Of the apse.

Short, playful glissandos and trills
Scattered judiciously
Throughout the rill of sound,
Streaming over the grove
Of tables and chairs
Occupied by mesmerized aficiandos
Of the trio of musicians,
Cupped together in the intimate room
Dusked by the soft, dim light.

Save your rhapsodies for those
With unquenchable appetites.
I'll take a lilt, a wink,
And a walk-away.

A lacery of sharps and flats,
Of sculpted sound
Measure pauses
Of singing silence.

Waves of intonations
Sketched over and along each other,
Appearing in and out
At random lengths.
With no discernable melody—
An ebbing flow
From a dying master.

The music gave pause to her thoughts,
Like an elastic rubato,
Stretched with musing.

Within the slack strings
Silent songs wait
For the love
Of a tautening hand.

I transfer my music
From my voice to my feet.

Her voice, a crystal,
Hung in the air—
An angel's promise.

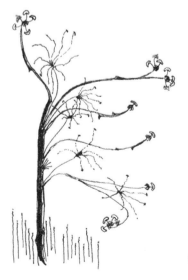

Young fingers
Mused thoughtfully
Through the etude,
Disguising difficulties
As rubatoes

Wisps of "La Mer"
Wafted fitfully
From tentative voices
In wave after wave
Of sighs

The choir murmured
A lullaby,
Gravely wakening
A drowsing Brahms.

Every Sunday at two o'clock,
His distant beloved voice
Bevelled the sharp edges
Of her loneliness.

So easy to imagine
The air astir
With a flock
Of Giotto's frantic fluttering angels
Studding a fresco sky
Above the field of Innocents
Set upon each other
By distant enterprising powers
Steeped in eager greed.

The engorged brush
Of the blind painter
Spat out
A roomful
Of Jackson Pollacks.

Feel the serenity and certitude
Of a Flemish painting
Bathed in shafts
Of rectangular light.

Bernini's columned arms
Welcome St. Peter's guests.

The blind painter, the deaf musician,
And the mute poet
Sat rocking their chairs
On the old porch,
And, oh, the conversation!

LOST ARTICULATION

Erase the usual march of certain hours
Replace all edges strung along the day
With shifting shadings washed along the shoreline
Of failing footprints in deserting sand.

No need for railings, clocks, or new instructions
To make your way along a plotted route—
The brochure that you seek for the journey you must take
Is not found within a pile upon a desk.

Lean into mists and clouds and airy musings
And feel the fall you counter with your balance,
The center of your spirit that will hold you
To the Listening point the Holy Silence speaks.

Forget the Eden in your head,
A dream that never was,
Because to know that it had been,
Alas, too cruel a loss.

Mountain, high mountain,
Of what can you tell?
Of the valley
Within your soul.

I sit here alone
Much companied,
Browsing through memories
Filling the seat beside me
In familiar ease.
Across the table,
Other faces
From places in the heart.
Beloved, all.

THE PRISONER
Gathering shadows of his future,
Cast by his past,
Prepare to claim
His new moments.
The crumpled ball
Of his "is—was—ever-shall-be"
Lies frozen
At permanent crease
In the pit of his stomach.

Sweet and sour moments—
The tang of old age.

She squinted her way
Through the whole process,
Thoughtful and selective,
To make for a gladdening interpretation
To come away with.

Memories of it
Always outshine any holiday.

The ill-fated search
For non-existent treasure
Unbeknownst, became an ugly blessing:
His work yielded a ready-tilled field,
Useful for those
With seeds in their pockets.

The tang of hidden irony
Disturbed the harmony,
The faint buzz of it
Perplexing the small ensemble
Gathered at the table,
Silencing, suddenly,
The music of convivial conversation
With a shudder of stop.

Decisions, Decisions
While choices hang,
Nimbus-like,
Over their heads,
They go inside and dance.

You rob your idols
Of their humanity,
Who then float
Tractionless
In the temporary buoyancy
Of public acclaim.

So cleverly done by the few,
Merchandized for the masses
Thumbing a ride
On the newest brain of gadgets
To spew the latest trivia.

Get it over with.
Feel yourself past
Another dilemma,
Solution in hand.
Then . . .
Then what?
Another passage
Seen only for its grief,
The rest invisible
To squinted eyes
Below frowned forehead?
A throw-away life..
Ingrate!

Name them into life
Call forth the shadows
Name them into light,
Then lift the proper sword,
In clarity,
To defeat them.

The catastrophic nature
Of a casual gesture:
Atlas! Don't shrug,

When you don't know any better,
You do what you can't.

If you've never been awe-struck,
You're a fool.

When the spirit
Lies fallow,
In the stillness,
The small voice
Can be revived
By the devout listener.

When all flavor seems gone,
When the spirit goes blank,
Sand your cedar
And breathe,   deep.

A quick breath
Of sanded cedar,
And off you go—
Re-briefed with memories
To revive the journey's worth.

Mortalize the Immortal
To waft among us.
Awakened from Eternal Stillness,
The aroma of Grace
Leaps from the sanded cedar—
A promise.

The Tilt of the Mountain
How better to hone the spirit
Than the struggle of the climb?
How else to reach the crest
Of the devine?
The steep road calling on
Our mindfulness,
The rough path
That cleanses the soul
With Ugly Blessings.

Fallowness,
A reverent emptiness,
Abiding in full faith
For the new fall of seeds,
The spirit bared
In willing vulnerability.

Giddy with discovery—
Finally, the harbor within myself.
Land ho!

The quality of the gift
Is paid for
By the state
Of your mindfulness.

Gratitude
Makes gifts
Of it all.

In Lieu Of
I stutter around the missing word
Jarred from my stream of thought
With a clutter of awkward explanation
In search of
That precious bead of completion.

The brain may hold its course
While the mind careens.

He was tainted with an efficiency
Untinted by a humane efficacy.

Self-accosted,
In the deep recesses
Of a lonely mind,
Her mute appeal
Spoken through sad eyes
To ghosts of the outside world
Was a failed reach, as always.

The rootless Idea
Sought a niche in his brain
To irritate into life
A pearl of wisdom.

Another moment is registered
At the desk of consciousness,
Duly noted, checked off,
Then forgotten;
Stuffed willy-nilly into back rooms
Of the subconscious,
From which its invisible power
Commands and colors, untrammeled,
Our bewildering choices.

Burning with intent,
He burrowed into the idea,
Lighting, as he moved,
Caverns of increasing splendor,
Already scoped out
From earlier dives
He had made
Into the intricate stores
He had laid up
With each retreat forward.
Perhaps one day he would stay.

The unconscious never slumbers:
The private culture
Of the individual
That figurates continuously,
Every second of a lifetime,
Has answers to every "why"
The conscious mind asks
In the bewilderment of logic.

You have to know
When to keep your brain
Up your sleeve.

The effects of the incident
Reached his psyche years later,
Like the leading edge of light
Of some exploding star
From the distant past.

The idea, still in fetal state
With promises pending.

In failing constellations of thoughts,
A disputation of the soul.

Apology
Used as emotional blackmail,
Forced upon the wronged
To demand a proper spirit
Of forgiveness.

The silken roll
Of a complex act
Refined by mastery
Totters as in the beginning
In the requestioning of parts.

Night thoughts travel
On a re-oriented express.

A genuine oriental rug
Passed through her brain.

Despite the meandering nature
Of the ideas,
The snippets
Were sturdily hinged
Into one unfolding
Coherent thought.

The thread of ideas
Was firmly knotted
Into a period.

Halloween Mask
With the conscious mind
Acting in contradiction
To the brooding knowledge
Of the (behemoth) unconscious,
He could not remove the mask.

The strong tang of the Succinct,
Once tasted,
Then spreads at leisurely pace
Through the mind,
Unfolding afterthoughts
Tucked in the creases.

The sudden brilliant stream
Of the epiphany
Slowed to a measured pace
In the space in the brain
Set aside
For thoughtful musing—
For delicate examination
Lest its sense vanish
Like a dream,
When brought forth into the light of consciousness.

Let's get oxygenated here—
Think! Think!

You once again
Open the trunk
Of treasured threads,
Grazing your hands
Through loved memories.
Have you stopped weaving?
Come, give me your hand.
Let's find the way back to the loom.

Can't you write in Winter
As you managed in Autumn?
Are you leached so far
Of vital juices?
Look to your attic trunk
Of ubiquities once lively.
Brush them clear to older light—
A reconsideration
Of forgotten blessings.

A forest of ubiquities
Surrounded him.
With a blink of astonishment,
He re-vivified
Ignored blessings.

We cast our eyes backward,
Fiddle with our memories
To sing adifferent tune.

He pulsed a stroll through his brain,
An amble through memories
Impressionistically blurred
Through selective buffing.

The plumage of those years
Blooms brighter
In the nudging memory
Of drier years.

Unbeknownst,
We decorate our memories,
And rub with a friendly eraser.

You store Happiness
In an impregnable bottle.
In chosen moments
Open the closet door.
Take the jar down from the shelf.
Twist open the lid; breathe deeply;
But the contents degrade
With each such tampering,
So you lie longingly, nights,
Staring at the closet door,
Stagnated by memories.

From the fabric of that memory,
Nothing left but the lint.

From gathered scraps
Of long-gone yesterdays,
I fashion a quilt
For today.

Memories are tweaked out of recognition
Into new renditions,
Futuring the Past
In new duds.

Where am I going
And where have I been?
Do I turn the next corner?
To left or to right,
Or go right straight ahead?
If I slow down now,
Catch the light on the red,
I'll be able to wait,
Take some seconds to think.
With my memory back
Of my intended map,
Once again I'll have ventured
To store then to home—
But my groceries, alas,
I forgot.

The patina of long-held ideas
Clung to his future plans,
Obscuring the intent
And operation of them.

Our eyes sweep past all others
To bore into the enemy
Who bears our devotion.
The drill of focus,
The thrill of power
To lean into the point,
Fully instrumented to the cause.
(The joy of zealotry.)

Squint away your realities.
Let your lashes
Curtain your window
On the world –or
Blink rapidly or
Close your eyes –or
Turn from the window entirely,
Sink to the floor
Beneath the sill.
Do what you must!

Give a wary shudder of forethought
Before you unleash your tongue.

He lived his life
In the subjunctive,
Always in fear
Of "what if's."

If we knew, before hand
What we would see
Looking back from the other side
Of these these years, these days,
These moments—
How we might lean into those passages,
Breathe more deeply,
Catch a scent at its budding,
Stay with its flowering
As nourishing gardeners
Along the rows of weeks we are granted.

Eye lid fluttered,
The look skidded aside
From contact:
"I didn't see what I saw."

After the vacation
It was Monday every day
The following week.

Undone by self-sabotage—
And so skillfully,
So willfully.

I rummage through
The detritus of my experience
Lumped through with caliche
In the once-loamy-seeming days.
What to do with this aggragation,
This destroyed mosaic
Of incoherence?
Study its new language?
Or create it?
Or use it
For the ultimate gravity?

A rill of private thought
Led me away
From the main conversation.
When I returned,
The main sense of it
Had streamed by.
"What?"

It's the principle?
It's not the hunger?!

A pedestrian stick-to-it-iveness settled in
Once the harness was slipped on,
The daily oats accepted,
The carriage full of riders,
A rutted route deepened
By the wheel of Time.
An early-on weariness had never lifted
With enough energy
To wield any question.

I didn't want the book
On the scale with me
After all the trouble
Of shaving my eyebrows,
Plucking my lashes,
Taking out my teeth,
Then standing on one leg
When I got on.

It was like living with a dormant volcano,
Or over the St. Andreas Fault—
Sounds impressive
But is really boring—
All that waiting;
Though it now and again
Can add an imaginative edge
To a dull day.

In the press of pages,
Squeezed of love,
A given rose,
Its color a rust stain
Of its former blush,
Its softness
Now brittle to shredding
Like the ancient book
It nests in.

He felt a wobble of fear
Through his frame
Before the step onto the stage
To pour his spirit, committed,
Into the evil role.

My agenda
For the day,
Listed on a sheet of paper,
Didn't make it
Off the page.

A handy shrug
Hides the scramble of thoughts
She would unwind later.

The imagination of the ear
Works overtime
In the silence of an unfamiliar house,
In the darkness of night.

In what forest
Are you going to "find" yourself,
Bumping into trees
In the dark
With no identity?
If you're hiding from yourself,
Who's doing the hunting?
Are you sure these are the right trees?

How many messages
Was I dismissive of,
How many unrecognized gifts
Escaped the notice
Of a young brain
Luxuriating in creative ignorance!?

I read you, sir—
I read you in the flick
Of your eyes,
In the side jut of your chin,
In the swallow at your throat,
In the tap of your finger,
In the pump of your leg.
Still yourself.
     And you sir,
A sprawl on a couch,
A flop of hair,
A droop of the eyes.
A yawn of the mouth,
A scratch of the neck
A wrongly-buttoned, bunchy sweater.
Stir yourself.

He stood there gazing,
Full of appetite
And love.

Her skin murmured silently
Under his gaze.

I long to borrow
Tomorrow
For just an hour
Today.

Unbeknownst she left behind the
The treasure she went looking for

Wandering in a Shoe
I knew the shoe would pinch.
Eschewing comfort.
Instead, I fed
My vanity.

A Fragile Reality
The beauty clicked into place.
The proper distance once achieved,
I must sit and yearn—
Not dare a greedy step nearer,
Nor a backward step to its oblivion.

We tease, with flip tongues—
Bandy-about truth
That lightly brushes across our foreheads,
Warding off
The weightiness of its power,
Until the day
We have prepared
The depth
To receive it
Full strength.

If you're in a hurry,
Do it slowly.

If you're feeling the slipstream
Of the passing turtle,
You're slower
Than not moving at all.

The elephant in the room
Stood there in quiet decorum,
A look of bewilderment
On its face.

Everybody has an accent,
Depending on where they aren't.

The vinegar of life—
Sour on the tongue,
Nourishing to the spirit.

From behind your boat,
Wakes, no matter the scale,
Quickly settle to gone;
Don't look over your shoulder
In pride.

Acquaint yourself
With the web
Of your personal spider
Through opera glasses
Before you proceed

The short-sighted man
Was master of all he surveyed.

Such a shame—
A first blow
Into a pretty hankie.

At some osmosian point,
The teckkie
Turned into a robot.

The red alert
Of dead canaries
Unheeded:
We squint-eyed ourselves
To death.

Dr. Oz is too healthy
To ever die of a disease—
He'll probably succumb
To hug-a-cide.

When did you last blink in awe?

We are all citizens of the Universe
With every atom of our Being.

The obvious
Does not make it true.

Tweaking the finial
Won't get you any closer to heaven.

For the Unseemly Bored
Too ordinary?!
Think an "ordinary" acorn,
A whole tree inside,
With bark-y trunk and slender-er branches,
With years and years
Of thousands of kaleidoscopic leaves,
Twiggy nests built by "ordinary" birds
To domicile ordinary eggs
Of future worm eaters
And roots to grasp the ordinary soil
Tunneled by ordinary worms.
Oh, and you, an ordinary gleam/In a father's eye.

Burning up in the theoretical,
Hanging heavy
On a delicate web
From a too-early commitment
Too fiercely declared.

Take up the thread
Of what must be—
Recognize and honor it.

Enemies repeat themselves
In each other.

On a hot day,
The delicious wisp
Of a cool breeze.

As long as there is time
For a few more epiphanies,
The future lives.

Balance
When to streamline,
When to adorn.

A worldful
Of re-named Pandoras
With venal hands
At the lid—
Wasn't once enough?

The Fairytale of Perfection:
A stiff fit in Reality—
A machine in an organism.

Psychology wins out
Over logic every time
Unless you're a Vulcan.

Color in the given spaces
With institutional crayons,
Instructed to stay
Within subscribed lines,
The stipulated "creativity"
Of the suggestion box.

Choose your gauntlets wisely.
How many spares can you have?
(If you're a cat, eight.)

Ancient Greeks
Clarified their "Whys" about Nature
With emotionally administrating gods.

Ideology,
Pre-processed;
Align yourself
And color inside the lines.

Caustic Comment
A bit of acidity
Brightens the brew
With a living edge.

Don't make a mountain
Out of a knoll,
Continuing to lie there
Skewing your view.
Up on your knees!
Now unfold yourself tall.
You'll see that the problem
Will shrink itself small.

Little things
Beget and be-grow.

No oasis can mitigate
An inner drought.

The intensity of your passion or belief
Is not the measure of its truth.

First off,
Match your buttons
To the right button holes.

Don't flaunt a magnificent wake;
It's gone
Sooner than you can claim it.

When it's full of hypotheticals,
Watch where you skate.

Anthropologists don't sneer.

More than again: Still.

Your software
Isn't going to change
My hard drive.

Don't lend the tyrant
Your tongue
To speak his voice.

In some circles
Being interestingly nuts
Holds a certain cachet

No amount of wheedling
Can affect a foregone conclusion
It's waiting at the gate
Before you get there

Collectors gather up
Pockets of forgotten treasures
Coined in past negotiabilities
No longer current.
The boxes become dusty
On shelves never visited.

Unheeded Advice

Pandora! Don't!

Don't be a silly goose, Leda.

Forget it – Dionysus will never get sober.

Don't hang out with lemmings

Pandora's box remains ever open

Don't enthrone your feelings;
They can be easily usurped

He felled himself swinging at a gnat.

Adversity clarifies.

Just put it in a poem – and shut up!

Oh, the great temptation of a loose tooth!

The bored are boring.

The bored search not for meaning, but for
New sensation.

Extend the comfort zone
With pillows of familiarity

Forget the "what if's;"
The "is's" are
More than enough to handle

You want God to wreak your vengeance?!

May hard peas insult your bed.

A wicked elaboration obscured
The simple truth beneath
The placid face
That hid a rich wickedness of mind

Grace is bestowed, not achieved.

There's an epiphany somewhere in here.

Honor your gifts.

Clever but unwise.

They don't see; they project.

Don't make an insult a resident.

Those who abide
Do not tap the impatient foot
Of those who wait

If you weep
At what you reap,
Remember who did the planting.

Bright Lucifer
Makes his beguiling bid
Along every man's path.
Sometimes in a whisper,
Sometimes with a wink,
Sometimes in a Souza blare.

The eye of the child
Is different with awarenesses
Long faded by our careless use.

Slow down and let your life catch up with you.

As the shouts fade,
The whispers of truth
Hold sway
In the winds of promise.

Silence is a space
Must you fill it??

Nothing is more satisfying
Than a successful nap.

He can eke 4 out of 2.

God is not parochial.

Too often spoke
Becomes dumb in the ear.

People out there—
Atlas is shrugging!

I sit here alone
Much companied,
Browsing through memories
Filling the seat beside me
In familiar ease.
Across the table,
Other faces
From places in the heart.
Beloved, all.

You can practice insouciance
In this jacket.
The soft-draping material
Easily submits to body topography,
With pockets to cup lazy hands,
Perfect for the gentle slouch
Of indifferent contentment.

Strideful with pride,
Overriding hesitation
Over flaws
In the pathway.
Skimming over niceties
And drudgedies alike.
The canopy of the sky
Unblemished, cooperating,
Volunteering the brightened ambiance
To prove the optimistic soup.

Mesmerized in normalcy as we are
By the slow, deliberate techtonic breathing
Of our everydays,
The casual shrug of an Atlas-like adjustment,
Jolts us to recognition
Of an ever-present underlying reality.

Once unseated from familiar anchor,
The tug of a new gravity
Set loose a nomad in her brain
Never suspected, and untravelled.

Nudging reminders
Itch in my brain.
Nag nag nag

At some trigger of words
Along the stream of conversation
She left off hearing it,
And started listening
To a branching rill
Of her own inner voice.

Out to pasture,
Eating the rag-weed of old plots—
It ends before it ends.

All my contentiousness
Is in my head,
Not on a real battlefield
Strewn with rumpled clothes
Filled with the dead.

The lights go out when she leaves the room
With never a hand at the switch;
The next one brightens at her step—
She takes day with her.

For the last time
She slid closed the arc of the desk cover.
Hollow-eyed cubby holes,
Shadowed in darkened emptiness,
Nested behind.
At her feet,
Filled with scraps of past negotiables—
History in a basket.

The bridge up,
Surrounded by a moat
Of quiet evening thought,
Comes the click of coherence
That orders the collage
Of the day.

I feel like a newly-tilled field
Aroused by the jolt of triggered seed;
A continuum of reconfiguring shapes
Moves within my furrowed brain.

He nods his way through the day—
A half-asleep yes-man.

The strained conversation
Thudded to a halt.

The stay of reality
After the blink of fantasy.

Tweets and tweaters chirp
From the lips of dignitaries
Going out on a limb
With commentaries
That ruffle the feathers
Of listening bird brains.

He wag-tailed directly toward me,
Fresh from the kitchen beanery;
"Out, out stinky Spot
(Shakspearean Doggerel)

At the Airport
I swear, Sir,
I'm a grandmother—
It's play dough.

The thing sits dumb,
Solidly unkenetic,
The energy mockingly locked
From my access,
Two pages short
Of completion.

The laying on of dust
Unmarked by human print-
Time's quiet claim,
The patina of isolation.

She spent her summers
Wintering where best she could.

The prodding nurse
Said I had beautiful veins,
Performed her task
With an easy slip-in.

He was gone
But his title intact,
Speared by a tack
On the bulletin board:
"Position open."

A jerk on the line
Reminds the kite
Of its conditional freedom.
Mastering its movements
Gives us recompense

Some day I'll drive off
Without my car keys.

It takes a whole armory
To open up a package.

Words—silkened in pretension—
Slide past and off
Before a call for meaning
Can snag them.

Your "sorry"s are a burden
That add insult to the pain.
I must extend assurances
That everything's O.K.
Which uses up my energies
To lie, resentfully,
And be reminded of the lie
Each time I see your face.

Possibilities abound
At the hands of the Ignorant,
Who don't know
It can't be done.

The glittering shallowness
Out-bid the steady glow.

All of my sisters
Have had toe trouble.
Being the oldest,
I must have used up
All the good toes.

The Madonna of the Cafeteria
Tucked beneath tilted head,
In a cradling arm
Nests a pink child
With a waving foot.
Two bags on a neighboring chair
Are bountifully stocked
With toys and a sweater
And bottle and diapers
And ...   and . . .
And. . .   and .

The patina of crust
On the highchair,
Sticky floor beneath,
Wanton smears from icky hands on clothes,
Colorful palette around the mouth;
I'll get it all,
After I wash his face.

An assembly of girdles
Were squeezed in old-timey discomfort,
But on their faces,
A learned stoicism.

At whose table
Were you served the brew
That warmed
That comforted
That exhilarated
That marshaled your imagination
Every afternoon
At five o'clock?

Beloved Visitors
They lie sleeping in my bed
In a room
Down the hall.

I lie awake
At the other end
On a comfy couch,
Contemplating treasures
At two in the morning.

The door had something to say,
Its squeak rich with waiting.
The rare performance
Spoke of his return from long absence.

I empty myself of false deferences
Like with old files—
Luxuriate in the space released
From jetted flotsam.
The remaining motes,
Patina of dusty time,
Are cleansed from the newly-cast Air,
Pregnant with possibilities.
I hold still—-and steep,
In the relief of fallowness.
Foreign Energies stir.

A Tryst
I am pending-less
In this still moment,
Settled into
A complete arrival
Of Now.

Drifting thoughts
Lazed through her,
Bumped together into
Re-arrangements.

Legs leadened to cement,
She strained to turn the corner,
But could only twist forward,
Enough to glimpse her future
Walk away,
Touting a bag full of possibilities.

I breathe richly
In this streaming world,
Deeply in
And smoothly out.

A piercing focus
Burned its way,
Flared into an epiphany,
Then was gone,
Like a lost Eden.

A pocket of mood
Wisped across my day
At sudden corners.
I shook myself free.

Trapped in solemnity
Living from vow to vow
Ritualizing out
Any remaining juices.

Like the frozen flow of color
In veined marble,
Her thoughts,
Faint and paralyzed,
Settled from a long ago lassitude.

Ubiquities Revisited
They have slipped through a slit
In the veil of the subconscious,
Behind which,
Slumbering or brooding,
They await renewed attention—
Suddenly to brighten
Or taint
This day's imagery.

Seated in a small chair
At the small table,
I'm not waiting
I'm abiding with my thoughts,
That range uncorralled
Beyond this small space,
Into endlessness.

In the corridors of the mind,
Who can tell distorting echoes
From originalities—
From true voices?
They mingle
In blurring self-deception.
Before journeys end,
Pray for untangling
To make
Your last gesture.

Nostalgia:
A yellowed silken dress
With long beads
Exuding a hesitant fragrance,
Delicate, enchanting.

Tip-toeing through the microcosm
With a be-rimmed eye
At the lense.

He was a man of temperate climate,
Whatever the weather.

She was part of the furniture
Of the place,
A site of few words
Of acknowledgement
Or direction—
Seconds of vital exchange
On a blank social calendar.
"Who gave you this information?"
"A small desk
Left of the entrance."

She fronts her pain
With a smile,
Hoping it will back itself
Into her head

Even if it's not there,
I'll find it.

A drop of the eye, a blink,
A turn of the head
To deny realty—
He devises hypotheticals,
Never leaving the revolving door
In a final step.

She looked more encased
Than dressed,
No topographical evidence
Of shape or movement from within—
Face botox-solemn.

Third person to myself;
An in-house research project.

If I'm listening
For a cheery voice,
I chirp it
Myself.

She no longer has a life,
But a series
Of at-the-time
Life Styles-
A true fad fan.

She flowered one vase,
Shined some surfaces
To groom the room
Visitors would see.

He had the practice
Of sweeping his debris
Into the other guy's yard.

He stubbed his brain
On a cul-de-sac
He had mistaken
For a highway.

She managed a life
Resting on other people's laurels.

She lived her life
In parentheses—
Always an after-thought,
An almost missed aside.

She is a freeway
For other people's secrets,
But they still tell her.

Should I re-vamp vigorously,
Or fizzle out, as is?

Her Face Book laundry
Needs to be boiled
In a black cauldron
With a big fire under it!

She had made an investment
Of many smiles and more tears,
Taught by productive failures
Followed by blushes of achievement-
Modest peaks,
Quieted sadnesses.

She comes bearing griefs
With grace,
Ugly blessings
Fully seeded
With promised joy
By the counterpuntal hands
Of love.

She was packaging
Without content—
An eyeful
For the fantasy-besot.

He stubs his brain
Against the habit
Of a permanent detour.

Here he comes,
Bloated with negativity.
Run!

Like unannounced horse radish
On the tongue,
She appeared in the doorway.

He was a one-pleat, one key accordion.
"In the name of Thor's thunderbolt,
Will you please shut up!"

The words reared in her throat,
Spat out wildly
Hot as a blast furnace,
Then caught in the air,
Hung frozen in mortification.

Christopher- A Lover of Place
By the magic of stationary movment,
He flies the country to each site,
To interview, with drinking eyes,
Its mountains, valleys, forests, trails,
Riverways, lakes ocean shores,
Up to cloud-piled skies,
While I, though tethered by phone
To my desk,
Travel with him
Through the relish in his voice.

It takes him
More than one word
To say "No,"
Instead, postponing
With "We'll see."

I like whistlers
And squeaking rocking chairs.

His voice, bright with anger,
Crackled lightening.

At eighty
She picked up
Her brightness.

He had a slow ear
And a slower mind to it,
Mulling consequences
Either way.

Vickie—always a clarion call
To the next adventure,
So deeply felt,
Ever-ready,
Full of scripts
For us all to partake of.

He spoke in short, static barks,
Shards of sound
Hard to distinguish as language.
His fervor stuttered out of him,
Jerked his body
In emphatic gesticulations:
Semaphoring hands,
Nodding head,
Twitching eyes—
Words stormed out of him
Until he tottered against the dias
And slid to the floor;
His voice, too,
Slid off his rant
Into a bleat;
Then, silence.

His words bellowed and billowed
Over the crowd,
The very meaning blurred
By the blare
Of his megaphone voice.

He was direct, sincere,
Rawly ideological,
With no bridge of humanity
To temporize his steely faith,
No margin to gentle
The terrifying grasp
Of his blazing eyes.

He had a great power of gravity
No one in his horizon line could resist:
Instant satellites
Trapped in his magnetism.

I take it upon myself
To perceive messages
In every coincidence.

The false eyes
Grazed the scene lazily,
With controlled appetite.

The fabric of her life
Became richly brocaded
With threads introduced
By earlier investments
At a well-woven loom.

Charley
He crafted his life
With the chisel of his mind
Creating and burnishing
Love manifest

Between earthy indignities
She plied her shining spirit

In the magical floating room,
He extends the spell
Of his enchanted eye
To young drifting minds,
And prepares them
For further seas.

She wore out
The nature of surprise
With its constant use,
Spilling out the drama
To any who,
Eventually, would,
Supposedly,
Listen.

Cindy comes.
The evidence is clear:
The silent clops in the driveway
Appear and fade
With the tire marks.
Different lives brush past
In the morning stillness
Cindy comes.

Her Vesuvious mouth
Makes me quake
When I hear it
From under the covers,
Sopping with sweat
How I wish
They'd get along.

Her late-blooming,
Long deserved joy
Eased the suffering
Of those who loved her.

Her fluid loquacity
Drowned her point.

She was an irritating grain of sand
In the oyster shell of her childhood.
We were totallly unsuspecting
Of her glorious future.

She was a diligent gardener
With a copious supply
Of ever-ready seeds
To plant
At the slightest bend
Of your ear.

You bring the fittings with you,
A template born afield,
The careful construct
Carried as Agenda.
You nourished and embellished it,
The lifework of your years,
And brought to bear Particulars,
Too alien to work,
Too disjunct to the purposes
Of any other way.
When they resist
As you insist
The rightness of your cause,
The elders mock your heresy,
Aghast and in dismay.
"You worship at the feet , sir,
Of the idol you have wrought."

The smooth churn of days
Tripped and fluttered to a stop
For an Eternal second,
In which time
The execution
Of the slightest turn of view
Changed forever his world—
Set a different trajectory
Of his tiny track
In the uncaring Expanse
Of the Universe.

Let us interiorate together,
Fall into each other's eyes,
Companionably,
In this lonely universe.

Lunch Bunch – A Dedication

Oh, the brainery
Seated 'round that table!
The wit, the bright slice
Through delicious and judicious fare—
The melt of laughter
And the camaraderie
Over a rich repast
Of shared years,
The lacery of good-natured gossip
Breezed among us.
New tidings
Freshen old plots.
The continuing monthly serial
Ebbing and flowing
With the arsus-thesis
Of viccisitudes and joys—
The cadence of life.

With a diagonal slice
Of the hot baked potato,
It falls open,
Like to the middle pages
Of a book.
The initial gasp of steam,
The aromatic release
At the mash of the tines
Decorates the air,
Titilates the nostrils.
At the lifting of lids,
A cloud of various pungencies
Blossoms and hovers
Over the ladened table—
A gala performance!

Before me,
A pretty garden in a bowl,
An overture for the eye—
Green, orange, purple, white, red—
Sings a lively palette
As I munch and crunch
The crisp-textured delight
While writing its poetry
Between satisfying bites.

Tuna out of its element,
Sandwiched between the remnants
And make-over
Of waving fields of grain,
A couple of filches
From Mr. McGregor's garden—
All these displaced ingredients
Converged on my plate.
Voila!

Moved To Tears With Chicken Soup
With Home-made Noodles
Textured and fat with an amplitude
Which catches on the tongue,
A bountifulness never known with the canned—
The slippery slender kind
That smoothly slides off the lifting spoon,
Escaping to the broth beneath,
Waiting for your second try.

The best rendition
Of the tomato
Is as a sauce
Sprawled
Over a steaming pasta.

A CUP OF SOUP
To savor the flavor,
I eat so slowly,
My lunch spans over
A four-page read,
And a poem
From a muse in a cup.

CHICKEN-RICE AT THE LUNCH BAG
Do your magic, oh chicken soup!
I made my way, blurry-eyed,
From Timbuktu,
A never-before destination,
Where six layers of ocular drops
Were applied
To already-clouded eyes.
I joined the swimming horde
Of day-busy traffic,
Squinting at the stunning glare
From a suddenly-hostile sun.
All the way from there to here,
My haven,
I got the feel
Of incipient little old ladyhood.

The little cakes
In the bakery display,
Rococo confections.
How could I bear
To bite into such a pretty thing!

Her speech
Was full of confections:
"Sweet," "Cute," "Adorable,"
And traps of "Don't you think so?"

At lunch
I launched
My daily pen
'Twixt measured bites
Of food, for thought

The apron displayed
A colorful palette
Of the evening's dinner.

The overly sweet poem
Was saved
By an unexpected nut
In the chocolate.

Lunch for Sudden Company
She gave the languishing celery stalk
A sharp slap of icy water.
The dispirited lettuce a strategic trim
The wrinkled carrot a clean shave,
And the sagging spinach,
A sprinkle of dressing
Bowled the stuff
And gave a blessing

A tasty morsel of words
Decorated her palette
As she chewed on the idea

A bit of recreational eating
Can fill
Different kinds of Empty
With temporary repletion.

Let's make a memory
We can savor later,
Again, and again, and again.

The mystique of chicken soup
From tongue, to throat, to stomach
Performs a miracle in the brain
With the coziness
Of reading a book,
Tucked on a sofa beside the fireplace—
How does it do that?

Nothing beats the aroma of rain,
And an active, cloud-piled sky
To wipe away
The bleached-white glare
Of a relentless summer canopy;
Better the leaden droop
Of nimbus grey.

Nature's designer shadows
Displayed on transluscent drapery
Of sun-bright morning windows—
A lacery of leaves
Dance to an orchestra
Of wind.

Driftwood,
Twisted from the drama of the waves,
Beached and dessicated further
By sun and time,
Abiding and beautiful,
De-sanded and displayed
On the mantelpiece.

Around 3 o'clock the quail come,
Full-familied,
To feed on the largesse (philanthropy)
Of the olive tree in season,
The sight of them
A fair trade
For the stain of pits
Left on the tile.

Beetled gone
To welcoming soil,
En-graved and feasted on
With the eternal industry
Of Nature's re-cycle agents.

Desert Gardener
Her hair a twiggy nest,
She leafs through the day,
Plucks out burrs,
Breaks off dried-to-sticks limbs
Of bushes and trees,
To free the green lushness
Nested in the older growth
Phasing into brittleness.
Branches, broken by storm,
Hang on the paloverde
By jagged edges.
She wrests them loose,
Drags the thorned wood
To a growing stack,
Leaving a tendrilled trail
In the desert dust.
Scratchy business—
Even through gloves and long sleeves,
Stained by the sap of vegetation,
Snagged by desert claws.
Hands and arms nicked in red,
With variously-dated scratches
On the mend—or not.
With tugs at leg tendons,
She steps up and down
Sloping walls of the wash,
Winnowing her way through thickets,
Alone in the familiar company
Of the desert.

The bespeckled fledgelings
Bore their spotted youth
With innocent abandon,
Open-beaked and expectant.

The Wind
Conducts clumps of cumulus
Streaks of stratus,
Misty cirrus,
Across the heavenly palette.

The slow-moving reflection
Of sky
Converses in the pond
With the gently-breezed ripples
At the surface.

The poetry of the yard
Is the willow in the back.
It shimmers in the sunlight,
Lacy branches dance the wind
And rustle their own music.

October
Somewhere the trees are brilliant,
A last gala flash accumulated
In compensatory glory
For the winter to come.
Make every last leaf count
Before it exhausts itself to sepia,
And loses its cling
In the winds of season.

At the curve of the season,
My senses revivify,
Relishing in anticipation
The changing palettes.

In the field, now fallow,
The earth finally breathed deeply
Past its exhaustion.

REVIVIFYING CURE
The clatter clutter in my head
Needs serious Spring cleaning.
No matter late into the year
I'll do it while I'm raking leaves,
And take it from the tree,
That shaking loose,with windy help,
It's best that time to do it,
So while it's gusting at my back
With motivating force,
I'll take the preparation course
That Mother Nature teaches.
'Mong newly-minted greenery,
To bud and bloom a fledgling batch
From branches stark and rested.

The dust eddied
In gritty, eye-biting swirls.

The Roads Taken
They met on a pathway across a field
Yellowed with shasta daisies.
As they strolled in the gently-warmed April,
The myriad strands of their separate wendings
Twined like a double helix,
Crystalized to a Tiffany glow of first love,
Then fired to the obsidian Of a "forever" vow.

Their gazes shifted and lifted ahead
To a highway smoothed to the horizon
With promise.
As their steps quickened
To a determined hurry,
They glanced less frequently
At the beloved along side.
Their mindfulness strayed,
And they found themselves
On a narrowed street,
Pot-holed with daily doings.

Their heads swiveled toward each other,
Faces distorted with disappointment,
Demanding answers.
Words like broken glass,
In the mouth,
In the ear,
Crunched underfoot
In the alleyway.

She sailed a smile
Across the room
Which he caught
At the edge of his eye.
With a crisp turn of head
For a surer look,
He sealed their fate.

Sequestered in the alcove
They warmed
With words of love,
They conjured a future
That dissipated, when they left,
By the end of the block.

The couple cast smiles
Across the candled table
On a Saturday night.

Reining in her unruly anticipation,
She tamed her trembling
Before she raised her hand—To knock.

Not a word nearer—
Not a wink nor a shrug,
Nor a smile nor a frown,
Nor a wave, not a slap,
Kick, rub, moue, kiss, tickle…
What does she mean?

Since he met her,
His life was a palindrome:
He never knew
If he was coming or going.

No need
For imagination's bliss
When I see you
Standing in the garden.

She loved him in her imagination,
Slotted him in the time and place
Of her need.
He complied—
For a short run.

To serve and save their love,
They parted,
 Recognizing the banality
Seating itself at the daily table
With a slice of toast, half cup of coffee,
Then the fleeting kiss of the day.

He was the iconoclastic bull
In the china shop of her life;
He oblivious to her vulnerabilities,
She to the precariousness
Of her invitation.

Her predilection
For petty pecking
Flaked off
His initial admiration.

The shared clamour of the past
Moved disturbingly
In daily silences.

With every movement
Of his jagged personality,
He shred her dreams.

With every denial of the reality,
The dreamer created
Someone else's nightmare.

Her house of cards
Destroyed a whole deck
Of efforts
Before the game was over.

The knot in her stomach
Got the message
Before her frozen brain
Grudgingly conceded.

Home was gone away from home
By the time I got back.
You had taken it with you
Along with my heart,
From the chest
Stored at the foot of our bed.
Why had I not known?

In The Dark
Her fingers were well-acquainted
With the braile of his face.

After the Corinthian flair
Of our affair,
We settled into plain Doric solidity.

The wedding,sadly,
The best day of the marriage.

The Promotion
He placed the arrogant champagne bottle
Onto the crumbed clutter
Of the table,
A swirl of grograin ribbon
Still flagging it festively,
Then emerged from the kitchen
And called up the stairs.

She found out
From a crumpled wad of paper
That had missed the basket
And lay on the floor beside it.
That's how she found out.

Sigh. How often we run past
The point of joy
To glean happiness
Only in retrospect.

The Dancer
We began our journey
In a disjunct tandem
At a freshie mixer in Kent,
He smoothly graceful
With field-practiced legs,
Flaming feet nimbly crossing
Lined yards or dance floor,
Swivel-hipped in a swing step,
Or gliding in a waltz,
Cradling arm
Guiding my fumble-footed,
Unaccustomed movements.
In stages increasingly refined
To matched rhythms,
We continued our dance.
Now, in latter days,
In a new balance
We cup elbow in hand,
Hand to elbow, like sistering beams,
The combination doubling our strength,
My steps sure, backward,
To his rubber-legged, tentative,
Testing forward,
Destinations to and from the bed,
A choreography of love.

"I shall return"–
The first promise
Of sixty quick-silver years

The $7.00 ring
Worked for fifty-eight years—
A lovely bargain.

But for the crackling of the paper
In his trembling hand,
But for the fallowness of his face,
You'd think him there in full person,
Despite small, continuing departures.
Yet, when his head
Edges toward his shoulder,
His eyes closed,
Paper lowered to Stillness,
I am reassured,
Because I do that too,
Nap in that chair.

The words could be mere scribbling,
Or plumbing instructions
Or an ornate delving into the mysteries of the universe.
The tilt of the head (The head knew to tilt)
Allowed the practiced gaze to fall upon the page.
The hand though trembling,
Held the volume in accustomed posture.
The rest of the body obeyed the cradling chair
"What? The title you ask?
The Vanished Man"

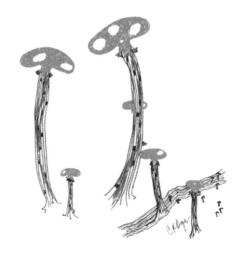

The trembling hand held the book.
Words on the page jittered
Before once-eager eyes.
The beloved object,
So tactile, so unfathomable
So lately graspable to the brain,
Failed to reach
The mind.

I knew he was leaving,
Along with his memory,
At the first missing gesture:
A touch of my cheek, and
"Good night, my love."

Would That I Could
A sadness hangs—
A cloud not to be lassoed
And dealt with.
No words can dispel
The drifting fog
You live in,
My darling.

The dying man
Semaphores gesticulations
Played out over the bed clothes,
Eyes closed to a private chamber,
And like a conductor
Before a small ensemble,
Directs final cadences.

It waited in the darkness
At the end of the hall
For him—who had wandered
From himself.
Under his reaching hand
The chair rocks, it pivots—
The earth tilts,
Disappears from his lean.
The chair settles, its back casters
Up against a table of tired plants.
Tipped on to front casters
It finally stills,
Looms over the prostrate figure
On the floor,
Unceremoniously cast there
In the dark.

IN MEMORIAM

In the inexorable roll
Of the Immensity,
The slip over the horizon
Of the once-shimmering space
Is sudden.
The empty space travels
And settles among us
Who stand blinking
At the dearness gone,
Never quite clasped
In the crowdedness of life
As we would now clasp
In the fullness of loss.
How few of us,
Timely gifted in recognition
Can now savor
Memory as enough—

The last consciousness—
Will you know?
Will you drape it,
Smother it
With your veiled mind,
To the insouciance
Of the last shrug,
Slip into oblivion?

Seeming tugs of distractions
In her zigzagged journey
Jolted into coherence
In the retrospective gallery
Of pictured memories,
As she lay
In her last bed.

Sentience gone,
The spark of life
Fled the body's indigence,
Returned to the magnetic universe,
A Familiar of stars.

The Waiting Box
There's a special box of words
That waits her description.
I feel it in a bright corner
Behind a door I haven't opened yet.
When it's time,
I'll clear a space
In my mind
For the poetry of her,
Then bring it out.

What words
Hover in the air
Above the silent lips,
Too late launched
By a failing brain?

Bob's mom died
Last night—early morning—
Sitting in her favorite chair,
Glasses newly laid
On the table beside her—
The book she had ventured through
Beside the glasses—
Hands tucked beneath lap blanket—
Settled into eternity.

In the chest
Among blouses and other garments
Was hidden a stack of templates
For every occasion,
Established early on
By close observation
And rote application.
Thus she mazed her way
In a world alien to her nature.
In the end,
Her store provided
The template-chaptered contents
For her book:
Etiquette and Safety for Martians.

Someone or something unrecognizable
Claimed most of the air
In the room
As its rightful cave.
She took a short, careful breath,
Hoping that her use
Of what was left
Went un-noted.

He moved relentlessly single-stringed
Through a life un-brocaded
By the variegatedness
Of most human experience:
A stunning starkness of mind,
Purified of humanity,
Deadly with focus.

Doors and windows sealed,
She was trapped with the tiger
Within her head.
She had only to strip the tape
And turn the knob,
But geared as she was
To the chaos within.
Outside was a fairytale
She once had dreamed.

Once upon a time
The world was flat,
Until a handful of fools
Braved the edges
And bent them
To undermeet,
In an unprecedented
World-wide hallucination
That is now unfolding itself
Back flat!
I told you!

She scribbled as fast as she could
To cover the baleful stare of the wall
Without examining
The nature of the ink she was using
To apply still another coat,
Stirred by an urge
Nested in a dark cove of her subconscious
To obliterate still another thrust
Of the same, persistent reality.

The bristling silence
Spoke only
Through the eyes
Of the hate-ravaged face.

Housed in a bewildered silence,
Unwise to take any dare,
Look into any shadowed corner
Or down the long hallway,
Or up the twisting staircase
Of his immediate memory.
We waited for the click
Of Time's camera
To shudder him loose
From the flat, eternal moment.

Hard Nights
Hooligan re-runs loosed
Up and down corridors of my mind—
I knock on doors
Which burst open
With new floods of old plots,
Joining in the melee—
Trapped on the thirteenth floor

Crawl up the side
Of the canyon wall.
Fall back again and again
Into the narrow, winding pit
Of dreary re-runs
In the vulnerable wee hours.

The silence leaned from all sides
Against my body,
As to absorb me —- gone.

Gone like a melting wafer
At the tip of my tongue.

Interrogate away!
I was never a Martian.

The padding of paws
Through thick wet foliage—
A sound she had brought back with her;
An alien parody
Of her clicking heels
Against cement pavement.
Would the echoing beast
Never vacate her brain,
Or had she too willingly
Penned the memory
Of her foreign enchantment
To an indelible imprint?

He complains
Of being stalked By Canadian deer
When he visits in Argentina.

With a neck-wrenching
Over-the-shoulder
Point of view—
She kept tripping ineffectually
Into each day's future,
Confused by the family strangers
Living in her house.

He could not escape
The hurtling voice
Still resounding over the years
From that vulnerable time
Such things inseminated his psyche
To be forever borne
As born to his Being.

It's as if I got on the wrong shuttle
To an unintended airline,
Lined through
To a gated community
Headed for an unknown destination—
All of us.

The lumbersome brain
Of the puppet-head
Waited for the ventriloquist's
Life-giving whisper.

I took my interestingly-creaky door,
Jamb, hinges and all,
To the radio station
To audition
For the Halloween night program.

In the bowels of Eternity
We tick our tiny clocks.

What the Marionette Didn't Know
The Marionette
Didn't know
About the strings.

The burning tongue
None-the-less
Continued the flaming words
The streaming eyes, the while
Clenched in denial
Failed to quench
The consuming truth

Fertile disruptions
Burst along the rows,
Raining nourishment
Deep into hidden crevices.
The simmering pools
Wait their time.

Once peopled,
A ghostly crew of chairs
Now draped in silence,
Abides
Around an empty table.

Voices linger
In the imagination
Of one who had once feasted there.

On Mars, we'll all be aliens.
When we landed,
Long awaited though we were,
Never-the-less,
The natives were astounded.

Leaves
Papery and crackling
Rustle on the deck
In a chatter,
Herded by the wind

The seasoning of woods
Spiced with yellow and orange and red and brown—
Wind-shaken from trees
To the floor of the bowl—
Is a savory for the eyes.

Wave after wave
The leaves drift and drift down.
My arms flat to my sides
Like a salmon against the current
I look up and swim to the sky
Past branches of still-remaining lacery.

I would like to acknowledge the support of those who did close reading of my work, made knowledgeable commentary, and convinced me it was poetry I was writing: Marilyn Buehler, Frank Dallas, Timona Pittman. and Joan Thomas.

Cynthia P. Dyer, my editor, and Jillene Enniss, guided me through the technical shoals to publication.

C. R. Dyer

Made in the USA
Middletown, DE
29 October 2018